Johann Sebastian

BACH

D1608525

BRANDENBURG CONCERTOS

VOLUME II

transcribed by Max Reger

FOR ONE PIANO/FOUR HANDS

K 03028

CONCERTO No. 4

J. S. BACH

BELWIN MILLS PUBLISHING CORP.

CONCERTO No. 4

J. S. BACH

9

302b

CONCERTO No. 5

CONCERTO No. 5

40

42

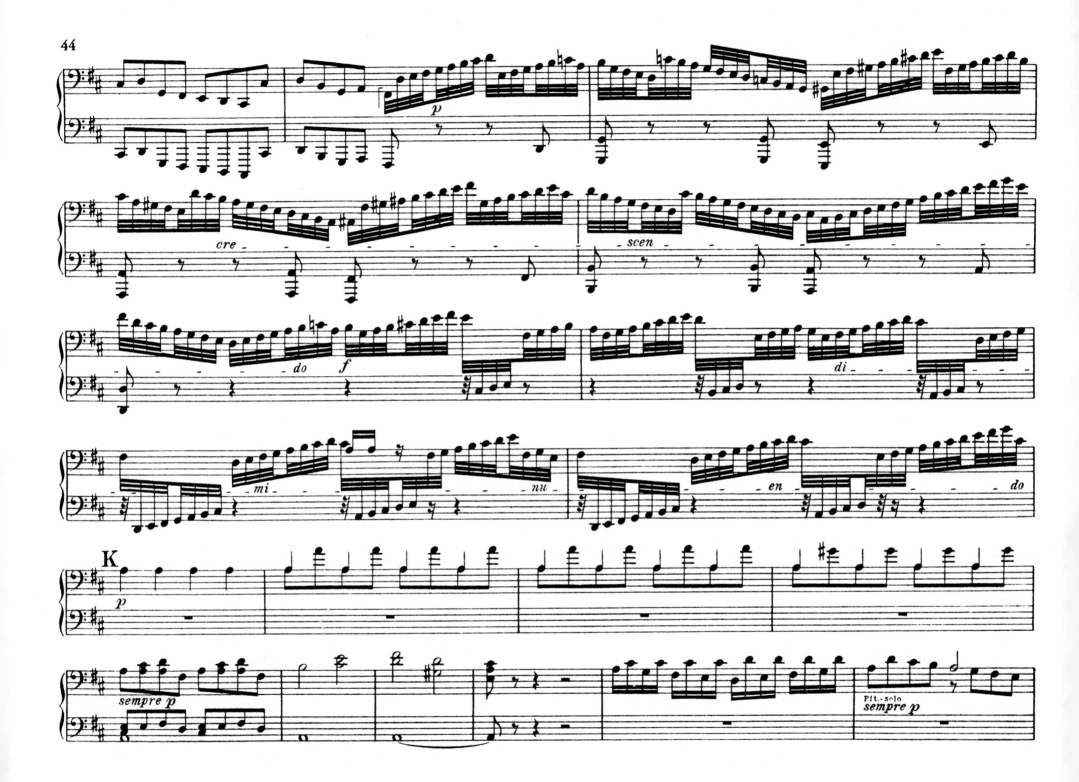

Affettuoso.

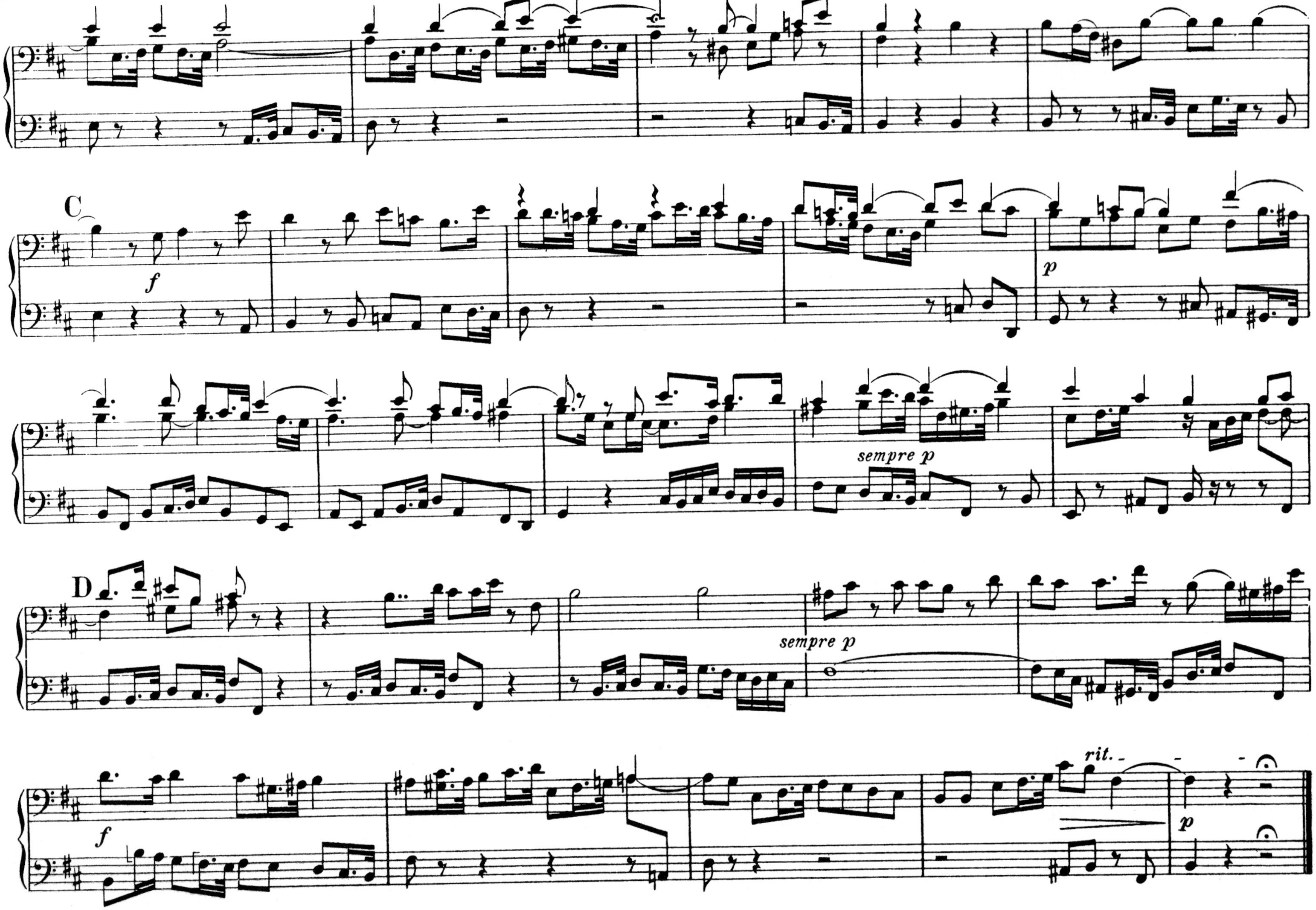
C
f
p
sempre p
D
sempre p
f
rit.
p

56

CONCERTO No. 6

CONCERTO No. 6

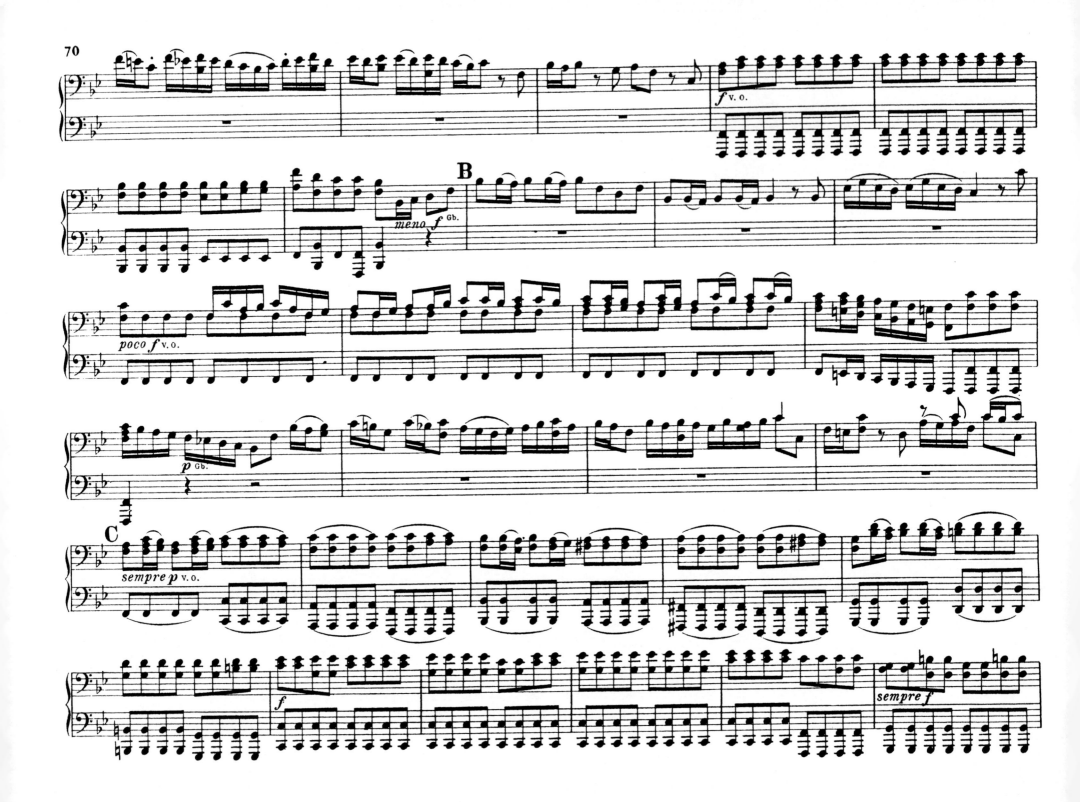

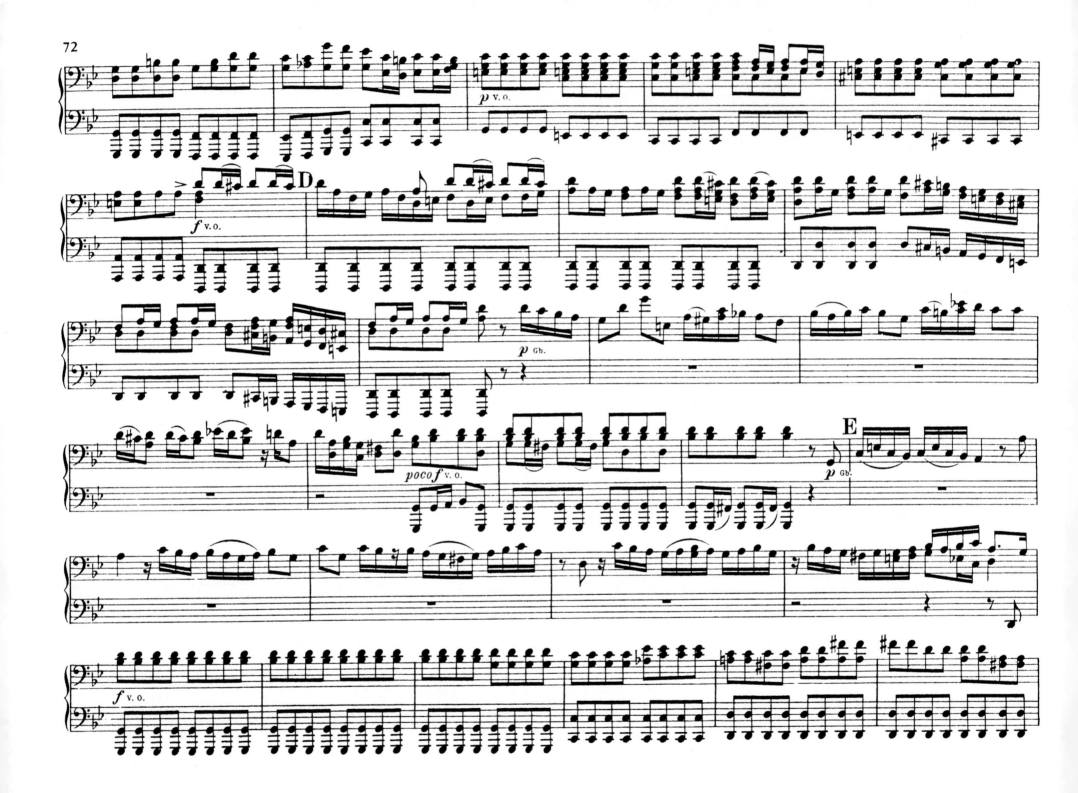

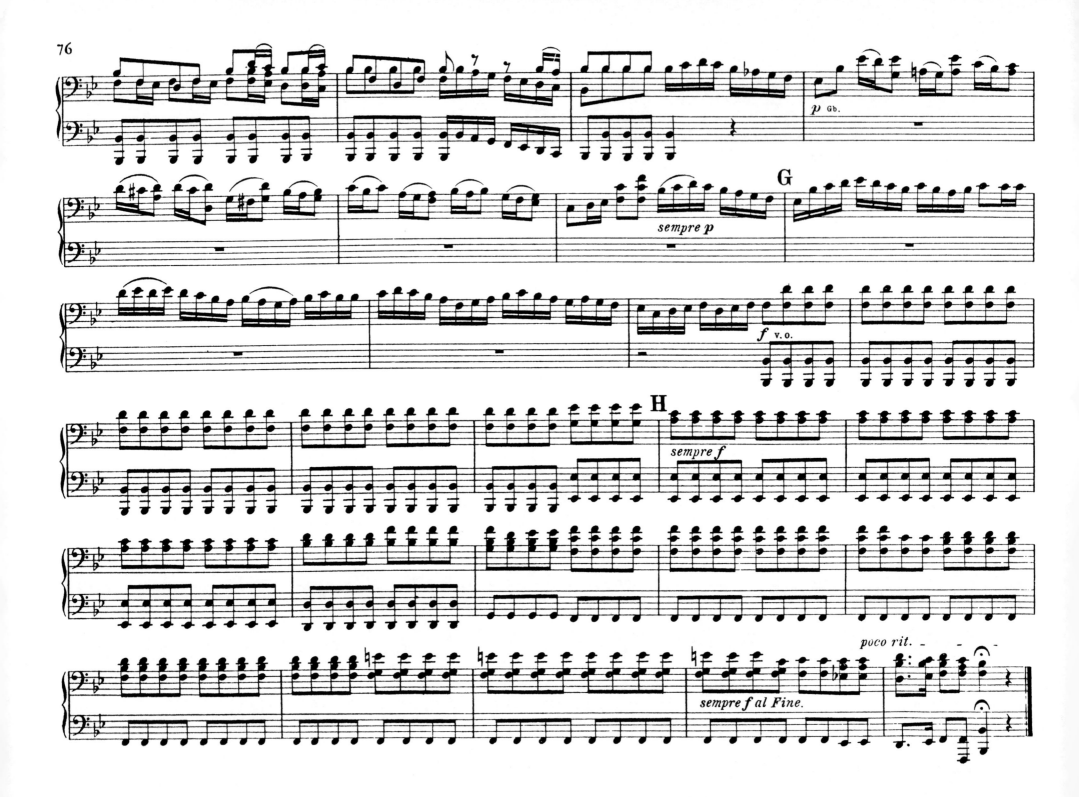

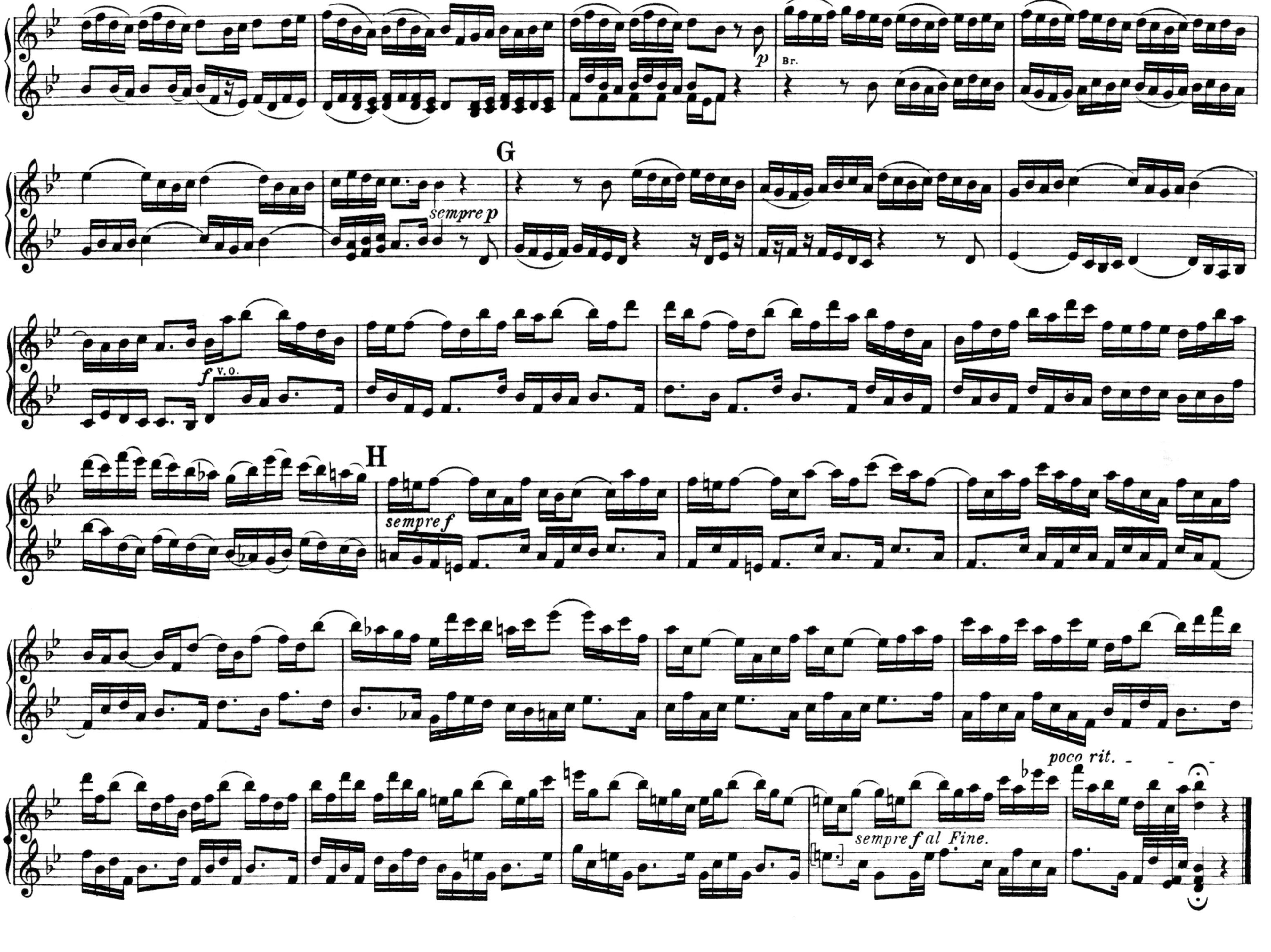
p
Br.
G
sempre p
f
V.O.
H
sempre f
poco rit.
sempre f al Fine.

Adagio ma non tanto.